NEW HAMPSHIRE
The Granite State

★

TEN TOP FACTS ABOUT NEW HAMPSHIRE

★ ★ ★ ★ ★ ★ ★ ★ ★ ★ ★ ★

•State nicknames:	The Granite State, The Primary State
•State motto:	Live Free or Die
•Capital:	Concord
•Area:	9,279 square miles
•State flower:	Purple lilac
•State tree:	White birch
•State bird:	Purple finch
•State insect:	Ladybug
•State amphibian:	Red-spotted newt
•State song:	"Old New Hampshire"

For my White Mountain hiking buddies: Eric, Julie, Brian, Megan, Christian, and Johnny. Stick up! — EC

Photo credits:

p. 4: U.S. Mint; p. 5: (top and bottom left) North Wind Picture Archives, Alfred, ME, (center right) Bettmann/Corbis, New York, NY; p. 6: The Tuck Library, New Hampshire Historical Society, Concord, NH; p. 7: (top left) The Tuck Library, New Hampshire Historical Society, (all others) North Wind Picture Archives; p. 8: Underwood & Underwood/Corbis; p. 9: North Wind Picture Archives; p. 10: North Wind Picture Archives; p. 11: (top) Superstock Images, Jacksonville, FL, (bottom left) North Wind Picture Archives, The Tuck Library, New Hampshire Historical Society; p. 12: (top) The Tuck Library, New Hampshire Historical Society; p. 13: (bottom) Corbis, (top right) Superstock Images; p. 14: (bottom) Corbis, (top right) North Wind Picture Archives; p. 15: (top) The Tuck Library, New Hampshire Historical Society; (bottom right) G.E. Kidder Smith/Corbis; p. 16: (top) K. Fleming/Corbis, (bottom right) J. McElholm, Single Source, Inc., Oxford, MA; p. 17: Kindra Clineff Photography, Winchester, MA; p. 18: (top) Kindra Clineff Photography, (bottom right) F. Grehan/Corbis; p. 19: (top) J. Sohm, ChromoSohm Inc./Corbis, (bottom) AP/Wide World Photos, Inc.; p. 20: (top left) AP/Wide World Photos, Inc., (bottom) Christa McAuliffe Planetarium, Concord, NH, (top right) J. McElholm, Single Source, Inc.; p. 21: (left, top and bottom) J. McElholm, Single Source, Inc., (top right) Superstock Images; p. 22: (top left and right) Superstock Images, (center left) D. Muench/Corbis; p. 23: (top left) D. Hauser/Corbis, (bottom left) North Wind Picture Archives, (right) Kindra Clineff Photography; p. 24: Bettmann/Corbis (French), Brown Brothers, Sterling, PA (Frost), Bettmann/Corbis (Hale), J. Chenet/Corbis (Irving), Superstock Images (Pierce); p. 25: Bettmann/Corbis (Stark), Superstock Images (Webster), Mark Perlstein/TimePix, New York, NY (Shepard), North Wind Picture Archives (Wheelock).

Photo research by Dwayne Howard

All other illustrations by John Speirs

ISBN 0-439-22293-1

THE
Jim Henson
— COMPANY —

12 11 10 9 8 7 6 5 4 3 2 1   1 2 3 4 5 6/0

Designed by Madalina Stefan

Printed in the U.S.A.

First Scholastic printing, May 2001

NEW HAMPSHIRE
The Granite State

By Emily Costello

SCHOLASTIC INC.

New York Toronto London Auckland Sydney Mexico City New Delhi Hong Kong

A Celebration of the Fifty States

★   ★   ★   ★   ★   ★

   In January 1999, the U.S. Mint started an ambitious ten-year program to commemorate each of the fifty United States. Over the next several years (through 2008), they will issue five newly designed quarters each year.

   One side (obverse) of each new quarter will display the profile of George Washington and the words *Liberty, In God We Trust,* and *United States of America.* The other side (reverse) will feature a design honoring a specific state's unique history, the year it became a state, the year of the quarter's issue, and the words *E Pluribus Unum* (Latin for "from many, one"). The quarters are being issued in the order in which the states joined the Union, beginning with the thirteen original colonies.

   To find out more about the 50 State Quarters™ Program, visit the official U.S. Mint Web site at *www.usmint.gov.*

NEW HAMPSHIRE'S QUARTER:
The Old Man of the Mountain

   The Old Man of the Mountain featured on New Hampshire's quarter is a unique rock formation on Cannon Mountain. Visitors to the state can search for just the right position in the valley below the mountain to see the profile of an old man in the overhanging rocks. According to geologists, the 40-foot-high granite face (first noted in 1805) was created when an ice sheet melted and slipped off the mountains more than 10,000 years ago. Today, cables and turnbuckles stop the rocks from slipping and destroying the formation.

   In addition to the profile of the Old Man, the quarter bears the state's motto: Live Free or Die. The phrase was coined by John Stark, a Revolutionary War hero. Some people think that short phrase perfectly describes New Hampshire's residents, who have the reputation of being as independent as granite is hard. The nine stars opposite the Old Man's profile represent New Hampshire's place as the ninth state to ratify the U.S. Constitution.

Native Americans with hunted deer

Early Settlement

The first people to live in New Hampshire were Native Americans who settled there about ten thousand years ago. They had no written language so we do not know much about them, but we do know they hunted bear and deer. Archaeologists have found many of their tools, including some stone points they attached to the ends of their spears.

In more recent times, tribes of Algonquian-speaking Native Americans lived in New Hampshire. These included the Piscataqua, Nashua, and Ossipee. The women of these tribes grew corn, beans, pumpkin, and squash. The men built birch-bark canoes and went fishing on New Hampshire's rivers and lakes. When the winter snows piled up, the Native Americans wove snowshoes from flexible branches and strips of leather to make getting around easier.

Native Americans giving thanks for the first snowfall of the season

The first European to explore New Hampshire was probably Martin Pring, an English sea captain. In 1603, Pring and his crew of forty men sailed down the coast from present-day Maine to Massachusetts. They were searching for a shortcut to Asia to carry on their spice trade and were also looking for sassafras because people at that time believed the trees' leaves could cure colds. Pring did not find a shortcut or sassafras, but he reported seeing vast groves of trees and large populations of animals that could be hunted for their fur.

Building birch-bark canoes

5

England's Third American Colony

A few years after Pring's voyage, Frenchman Samuel de Champlain visited the New Hampshire coast. He mapped the area, as well as the coasts of what are now Maine and Massachusetts. Then, in 1614, a British man named John Smith led a whale-hunting, fishing, and fur-trading expedition to the northeastern United States. He named the area he visited New England, and in 1616, he published a book called *A Description of New England*. People in England read Smith's book with great interest.

Even the king of England was paying attention. In 1619, King James I and some British businessmen formed a group to promote settlement of New England. They hoped that the people they sent to America would ship gold and other treasures back to them. Two years later, the king and his partners granted six thousand acres in New Hampshire to Scotsman David Thomson.

Thomson and his followers set out for America late in 1622. They survived five months at sea and built a settlement called *Pannaway Plantation* near the modern town of Rye. Thomson's settlement was the third permanent settlement in America — after Jamestown, Virginia, and Plymouth, Massachusetts. The next New Hampshire settlement, the town of Dover, was founded by two brothers from London named Edward and William Hilton.

Also around this time, King James I and his business partners granted a large tract of land to an English merchant, John Mason. Mason named his land New Hampshire after Hampshire County, where he had lived in England. In 1630, he sent a group of colonists to the area, and they named their settlement Strawbery Banke, after the wild strawberries they found growing there. Strawbery Banke is now part of the city of Portsmouth.

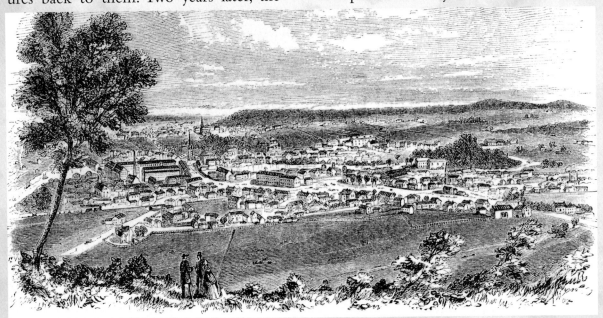

The settlement of Dover

John Mason naming his new land

Making soap

Minister John Wheelwright, left the Massachusetts Bay Colony in 1638 after arguing with his neighbors about religious issues, and then founded the town of Exeter. Another group of settlers from Massachusetts founded Hampton the same year. The colonists grew their own food, trapped animals, spun yarn, wove cloth, made soap, and dipped candles. Farmers had to work extra hard because New Hampshire's soil is rocky and the growing season is short.

Despite the settlers who came to seek their fortunes,

New Hampshire grew slowly. By 1640, the four New Hampshire towns had a total population of only about 1,000 — tiny compared to Massachusetts's booming population of about 20,000.

Clearing fields for farming

New Hampshire's citizens had a difficult time forming a unified government. A civil war in England distracted Mason from providing sufficient leadership. Unsure of their ability to protect themselves from unfriendly Native Americans and hostile French trappers, the New Hampshire colonists joined the Massachusetts Bay Colony in 1641. New Hampshire remained part of Massachusetts until 1680, when the king of England declared it a separate colony.

Spinning yarn

Busy trying to survive, and frightened by scattered bands of warlike Native Americans, the settlers had little interest in exploring the forests that surrounded their villages, let alone the range of snowcapped mountains farther north. Native Americans told the settlers that the tallest mountain, called Mount Agiocochook, was home to the Great Spirit. They said climbing it would mean death. In spite of this, an Irishman named Darby Field persuaded two Native American guides to follow him to the top in 1642. Field became the first European to climb what is now known as Mount Washington, the tallest peak in New England.

In 1652, John Endicott, then governor of the colony, sent a group of men out to search for the headwaters of the Merrimack River. The explorers, Simon Willard, John Sherman, Edward Johnson, and Jonathan Ince, became the first Europeans to locate New Hampshire's enormous Lake Winnipesaukee. The men chiseled the governor's name and their own initials onto a granite boulder now called Endicott's Rock. Europeans did not visit the lake again until 1736.

Early photograph of Lake Winnipesaukee

Trading with Native Americans

The French and Indian War

Over the next hundred years, New Hampshire's settlers carved villages out of the wilderness. They traded British goods with the Native Americans for furs and dried fish, cut down trees and used them to make ships for Britain's navy, and built dams in the regions' rivers so that they could have a steady supply of water.

The growing villages changed the landscape. As the settlers cut down trees, animals fled to find new shelter, and hunting became more difficult. Many fish died in the slow-moving, sawdust-clogged rivers. Soon there were fewer fish and animals for the Native Americans to catch, eat, and trade.

Meanwhile, the French had established trading posts to the north and west of New Hampshire. They wanted to take over the fur trade and were willing to fight the British for control of the area. Knowing that many Native Americans were angry with the way the British treated them, the French encouraged them to attack British colonists.

Over a seventy-four-year period, England, France, and the Native Americans fought four wars in North America. Many Native Americans were killed in battle. Others died from diseases they caught from the colonists. By the time the British won the French and Indian War in 1763, the Native American population was greatly weakened.

Battle between colonists and Native Americans

Revolutionary Leader

To help pay for the French and Indian War, England imposed a series of taxes on its thirteen North American colonies. However, the colonists did not want to pay these taxes because they were not allowed to send representatives to the British Parliament. "Taxation without representation is tyranny!" they cried.

Residents of New Hampshire and the other colonies began to talk angrily about breaking ties with England. On December 4, 1774, four hundred New Hampshire patriots raided an English fort near Portsmouth. They stole guns and ammunition from the armory and distributed them among New Hampshire's townspeople.

Four months later, when the Revolutionary War began in Massachusetts, hundreds of New Hampshire residents hurried to join the battle. One of the most important battles in the war was the Battle of Bunker Hill, fought in Boston on June 17, 1775. More than half of the two thousand soldiers fighting on the colonists' side came from New Hampshire. New Hampshire also built ships for the war. In 1777, one of these ships — the *Ranger* — became the first warship to fly the American flag.

While the war raged on, American political leaders began organizing a new country. On January 5, 1776, New Hampshire became the first colony to adopt its own constitution. Six months later, on July 4, 1776, the Declaration of Independence was approved, and the

Soldiers fortifying Bunker Hill, 1775

Signing of the United States Constitution

former British colonies became the United States of America. New Hampshirites Josiah Bartlett, William Whipple, and Matthew Thornton signed the Declaration of Independence in Philadelphia on behalf of their colony. The Revolutionary War ended five years later when the British surrendered in Yorktown, Virginia.

The newly independent colonies had a big task before them — creating a document that would describe the government of their new country. They agreed that the constitution would go into effect when two-thirds of the states accepted it. But it took state representatives twelve years to draft and adopt a constitution. On June 21, 1788, New Hampshire cast the deciding vote as the ninth state to ratify the document and enter the union.

Josiah Bartlett, first governor of New Hampshire

Matthew Thornton

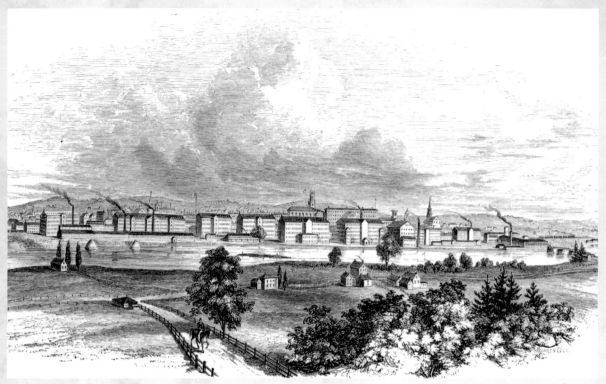

Factories in Manchester

Farmers and Factories

After the Revolutionary War, many of New Hampshire's residents turned from farming to manufacturing. By the early 1800s, the settlers had discovered how to use energy from the state's many fast-flowing rivers to power machines. These water-powered mills processed lumber and ground grain to make flour. The state's first factory for making cotton cloth opened in New Ipswich in 1803, and the Amoskeag Company in Manchester introduced a power loom in 1819. Textile mills were soon an important source of jobs in New Hampshire.

At first, the textile factories recruited farmers, but by the mid-1800s, the factories began advertising for cheaper labor overseas. Immigrants from Ireland, Germany, Sweden, Scotland, Greece, Poland, and Canada flooded into New Hampshire to work.

Textile mill

12

The Civil War

By the mid–1800s, America was growing quickly, and territories in the western part of the country had begun asking to join the Union. This growth created a bitter battle over whether these new states should allow slavery.

Many Northerners wanted to outlaw slavery in all of the United States. New Hampshire had abolished the practice by the 1820s. But farmers and plantation owners in the Southern states relied on African slaves and their American-born descendants to do the hard work of harvesting the cotton crop, among other things. They were not willing to free their slaves.

In 1852, a New Hampshire native was elected to the White House. As President, Franklin Pierce, although pro-slavery, wanted to avert civil war and keep the

Franklin Pierce

Union together. His views about slavery were unpopular in the North and prevented his political party from nominating him to run for re-election four years later.

Civil War broke out in 1861 shortly after Abraham Lincoln became President. The citizens of New Hampshire were strong defenders of the Union. Nearly half of the state's male population fought in the war, and 3,400 New Hampshire natives lost their lives in the fighting. The North won the Civil War in 1865, and the country was soon reunited.

New Hampshire soldiers during the Civil War

Loggers

Mount Washington in the 1880s

Mills, Logs, and Tourism

After the war, the textile industry in New Hampshire continued its boom. By the early 1900s, the Amoskeag Company in Manchester was the largest textile factory in the world. At its peak the company employed 17,000 workers.

Logging was another important industry in New Hampshire. In 1867, the state sold 172,000 acres of wilderness in the northern part of the state to logging companies. They cut down entire moun-

Loggers guiding logs into rapids

Mount Washington Hotel

tainsides of trees and floated them down-river to paper mills.

These massive logging operations built highways and railroads that opened up the mountain area to tourists. Grand resorts like the Mount Washington Hotel sprang up in the valleys of the White Mountains. In 1911, the federal government created the White Mountain National Forest. Today, the forest has grown to about 800,000 acres — roughly the size of Rhode Island.

The heyday of New Hampshire's textile mills did not last long. By the early 1920s, mills in southern states began producing fabric more inexpensively. New Hampshire's mill owners cut wages, and workers responded by refusing to work. In the 1930s, the Great Depression hit. People across the country were too poor to afford many of the products made in New Hampshire's factories. By 1939, the huge Amoskeag Company closed down forever, leaving eleven thousand people in Manchester without work. Many New Hampshire mill towns suffered through decades of poverty and decline.

Abandoned factories

Concord

New Hampshire Today

Today those years of economic despair are little more than a bad memory. In recent times, more and more people have decided to make a home in New Hampshire. Between 1990 and 1998, the state's population grew faster than that of any other New England state. New Hampshire does not charge state income tax or sales tax. That means New Hampshire's workers keep more of the money they earn than residents of other states, making it a desirable place to live.

The tourist industry has thrived in the state, providing many jobs in the service industries. New Hampshire is a popular place to vacation year-round. In cold-weather months, resort areas like Cannon Mountain and Bretton Woods draw skiers. During spring and summer, visitors boat, camp, and swim in the state's 1,300 lakes. In the autumn, visitors flock to New Hampshire to see the beautiful fall foliage.

Sailing on one of New Hampshire's many lakes

16

Autumn in the White Mountains

Cross-country skiing in Bretton Woods

New Hampshire's factories produce machinery, food, wood and paper products, shoes, and computer, radio, and TV equipment. Many of these factories are located in the state's largest cities — Manchester, Concord, and Nashua.

In addition to its natural beauty, New Hampshire is well-known for the structure of its government. New Hampshire residents hold regular town meetings where citizens debate issues and vote on them directly. Social scientists consider this system one of the oldest and most complete forms of democracy in America.

Town meeting in Sandwich

Republican Party headquarters, Manchester

The little state of New Hampshire also plays a big role in the election of the U.S. President. Every four years, each state holds a primary election. In these elections, men and women who want to run for President of the United States seek the nomination of their political party. Since 1920, New Hampshire has always been the first state to hold its primary. Each election cycle, the eyes of the nation turn to New Hampshire as hopeful candidates travel to historic towns like Exeter and Dover to attract votes. Some say New Hampshire's role in national politics is too big. Others say that a state that played such an important role in U.S. history deserves nothing less.

John McCain campaigning in New Hampshire

Things to Do and Places to See

Christa McAuliffe

Christa McAuliffe Planetarium

Concord's high-tech planetarium is named for the resident who won a nationwide competition to be the first teacher in space. Christa McAuliffe's victory turned tragic in 1986 when the space shuttle *Challenger* exploded shortly after take-off, killing her and the six astronauts on board. The planetarium is dedicated to McAuliffe's dream — teaching children about space.

Christa McAuliffe Planetarium

Trained bear at Clark's Trading Post

Clark's Trading Post

Since 1928, visitors to the town of North Woodstock have stopped at Clark's Trading Post. First established as "Ed Clark's Eskimo Sled Dog Ranch," the popular tourist attraction started out as a place to raise and show Eskimo sled dogs. Owners Florence and Edward Clark brought bears to the ranch in 1930 as a way to draw visitors off nearby Route 3. In 1949, the trained bear show became a featured attraction. Today you can watch the bears do tricks, ride an historic railroad, dip your own candles, check out the Grimmy Family circus, see Merlin's Mystical Mansion, and more.

Covered Bridges

The back roads of New Hampshire are graced with more than fifty covered bridges. Built during the 1800s, these scenic bridges provided shelter for travelers during harsh winters, protected the road from collecting snow and ice that could make the bridge collapse, and helped control skittish horses by shielding their view of the water below.

Covered bridge, Jackson

A 450-foot span that connects Cornish, New Hampshire, to Windsor, Vermont is the longest, operative covered bridge in the United States. Other New Hampshire towns with covered bridges include Andover, Branford, Jackson, and Langdon.

The Flume

Franconia Notch State Park

In 1808, "Aunt" Jess Guernsey made a big discovery while fishing. The ninety-three-year-old woman came upon the

Old Man of the Mountain

Flume, an enormous gorge at the base of a mountain in New Hampshire's White Mountain range. Today, visitors to Franconia Notch can explore this natural wonder on a two-mile loop of trails. Signs along the way explain the area's geological curiosities and plant life. Don't miss the Sentinel Pine Bridge — a bridge built on top of a 175-foot tree that fell across the Pemigewasset River during a hurricane. Franconia Notch is also home to the Old Man of the Mountain.

Lake Region

New Hampshire boasts more than 1,300 lakes. Lake Winnipesaukee is the state's largest, with a shoreline 283 miles long and an area of seventy square miles. Winnipesaukee is a Native American word meaning "smile of the

Lake Sunapee

Great Spirit." Another well-known lake is Sunapee, near Claremont, where boats take passengers on relaxing cruises. Mount Sunapee State Park offers swimming and hiking in the summer and skiing in the winter.

Granite rocks in Lost River Gorge

Lost River Gorge

Save lunch for *after* your visit to Lost River Gorge. Eat too much and you just might get stuck in the "lemon-squeezer" — a boulder-formed cave just 13½ inches wide at its narrowest point. During the three-quarter-mile round-trip, you will have the opportunity to wiggle through several natural caves,

check out a sixty-foot-deep granite pot-hole with a twenty-eight-foot diameter, and see some lovely waterfalls.

View from the top of Mt. Washington

White Mountain National Forest

Tourists have been visiting the White Mountains of New Hampshire for more than two hundred years. The White Mountain National Forest is a natural wonderland of wilderness, scenic "notches" — valleys carved into the mountains during the glacial period — and rocky or snow-covered peaks above the tree line. The range covers most of the northern third of the state and contains spectacular scenery.

Mt. Washington is the tallest peak in the range and in New England. It is also home to "the worst weather in the world." The highest wind speed ever recorded on Earth, 231 miles per hour, was measured here in 1934, and the average annual snowfall is 177 inches. You can reach the top by hiking, driving, or riding the world's first mountain-climbing railway.

The Mount Washington Cog Railway

was built long before there were automobiles, electric lights, or telephones. The

Mt. Washington Cog Railway

train uses a system of gears that fit into racks built between the rails. Engines turn the gears and the trains climb the mountain tooth by tooth. The trains run on coal-fired steam, using a ton of coal and 1,000 gallons of water on each trip. The steepest section of the cog's trestle is called Jacob's Ladder. As the train climbs over this section of track, passengers in the front of the coach sit fourteen feet higher than passengers in the back!

Robert Frost home in Derry

Robert Frost Homes

The well-loved poet who wrote "The Road Not Taken" called New Hampshire "one of the two best states." (Vermont was the other.) The farm where Frost lived for eleven years is located in the town of Derry. Exhibits and films introduce visitors to his work. Another Frost home in Franconia is now a poetry center. A half-mile walking trail features poems to read along the way — some posted in the exact spot where Frost wrote them.

Strawbery Banke

Strawbery Banke

Ten acres in the scenic coastal town of Portsmouth have been transformed into a living-history museum named for one of the area's first settlements, Strawbery Banke. Explore three hundred years of New Hampshire history by wandering through forty-two buildings dating from the 1600s to the 1900s. Artisans demonstrate crafts such as weaving, pottery, and boat building.

Famous People from New Hampshire

Daniel Chester French (1850–1931)

Born in Exeter, sculptor Daniel Chester French made some of the country's most loved statues. *The Minute Man* in Concord, Massachusetts, honors the soldiers of the Revolutionary War who were ready to fight at a minute's notice. His masterpiece is the statue of Abraham Lincoln in the Lincoln Memorial in Washington, D.C., which took eleven years to complete.

Robert Frost (1874–1963)

Although America's most famous poet was born in San Francisco, Robert Frost attended New Hampshire's Dartmouth College and wrote most of his poetry while living on a farm in Franconia. One of his books of poetry, *New Hampshire,* is named after his adopted state.

Sarah Josepha Hale (1788–1879)

Born in Newport, Sarah Josepha Hale was the country's first female magazine editor. She edited and wrote for a magazine called *Godey's Lady's Book,* which was very popular with nineteenth-century women. She wrote the nursery rhyme "Mary Had a Little Lamb" in 1830.

John Irving (1942–)

Author John Irving, who was born in Exeter, sets many of his novels in New Hampshire. His best-known works are *The Cider House Rules, The World According to Garp,* and *The Hotel New Hampshire.*

Franklin Pierce (1804–1869)

Franklin Pierce was born in Hillsboro and

had an interest in politics at a young age. At thirty-two, he became the youngest member of the U.S. Senate. At forty-eight, Pierce became the fourteenth President of the United States. Only Theodore Roosevelt, John F. Kennedy, and Bill Clinton were younger when they took office. As President, he tried to deal with the thorny issue of slavery and prevent the Civil War.

John Stark (1728–1822)

Born in Londonderry, John Stark was captured by Native Americans when he was twenty-four years old. The Native Americans murdered one of his companions, but his captors liked the way Stark fought them without begging for mercy. They held him captive for four months and then let him go. Stark went on to become a Revolutionary War hero who played a key role in the Battle of Bunker Hill and the Battle of Bennington. He coined the phrase "Live Free or Die" in 1809. The phrase became the state motto in 1945.

Alan Shepard (1923–1998)

In 1959, the National Aeronautics and Space Administration (NASA) picked this East Derry native as one of the original seven American astronauts. On May 5, 1961, Alan Shepard became the first American to rocket into space. After this *Freedom 7* mission that took him to an altitude of 117 miles above Earth, Shepard commanded the third moon landing in *Apollo 14*. It was on this mission that he became the fifth man to walk on the moon.

Daniel Webster (1782–1852)

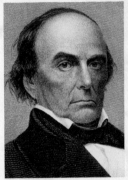

Daniel Webster was a great statesman, orator, and lawyer who was born in Franklin, then known as Salisbury. As a United States senator from Massachusetts, he tried to prevent the Civil War through compromise. He was against slavery, but he wanted the Union to remain one country. He served as U.S. Secretary of State under three different Presidents, argued many important cases before the U.S. Supreme Court, and was well-known for his eloquent, powerful speeches.

Eleazar Wheelock (1711–1779)

Unlike most early colonists, Eleazar Wheelock thought educating Native Americans was better than fighting them. He started a school and taught about forty Native Americans subjects such as Greek, Latin, Hebrew, and Bible studies. In the late 1760s, Wheelock moved his school from Connecticut to Hanover, New Hampshire, and renamed it Dartmouth after one of his financial backers. The number of Native Americans in attendance dwindled over the years, but Dartmouth remains one of the nation's most respected colleges.

White Mountain Memories

The White Mountains of New Hampshire have inspired travelers for more than 350 years. The following diary entries tell of attractions that still draw visitors today. The first selection comes from *The Journal of John Winthrop*, an account of New England life from 1630 to 1649 as recorded by the governor of Massachusetts. The second two selections include an excerpt from the diary of Mason Tappan and one from F. W. Sanborn's manuscript "How Frank and I Spent Two Weeks in the White Mountains of New Hampshire." Both original texts are housed at the New Hampshire Historical Society in Concord, and the observations of these ordinary men are published here for the first time.

June 8, 1642

One Darby Field, an Irishman, living about Pascataquack, being accompanied with two Indians, went to the top of the white hill. He made his journey in 18 days. His relation at his return was that it was about one hundred miles from Saco, that after 40 miles travel he did, for the most part, ascend, and within 12 miles of the top was neither tree nor grass, but low savins, which they went upon the top of sometimes, but a continual ascent upon rocks, on a ridge between two valleys filled with snow, out of which came two branches of Saco River, which met at the foot of the hill where was an Indian town of some 200 people. Some accompanied him within 8 miles of the top, but durst go no further, telling him that no Indian ever dared to go higher, and that he would die if he went. So they staid there till his return, and his two Indians took courage by his example and went with him. They went divers times through the thick clouds for a good space, and within 4 miles of the top they had no clouds, but very cold. By the way, among the rocks, there were two ponds, one a blackish water and the other reddish. The top of all was plain about 60 feet square. On the north side there was such a precipice, as they could scarce discern the bottom. . . . He saw to the north a great water which he judged to be about 100 miles broad, but could see no land beyond it. . . . When he came back to the Indians, he found them drying themselves by the fire, for they had a great tempest of wind and rain.

> — From the journal of John Winthrop,
> first governor of Massachusetts

September 26, 1844

We knew fortitude in finding a "guide" to conduct us hither in the person of a young gentleman . . . from Andover, Mass., who had been in the vicinity of the mountains for some days, sketching landscape views, and who kindly offered to accompany us. We visited "the Flume" first. This is approached by a foot path, worn

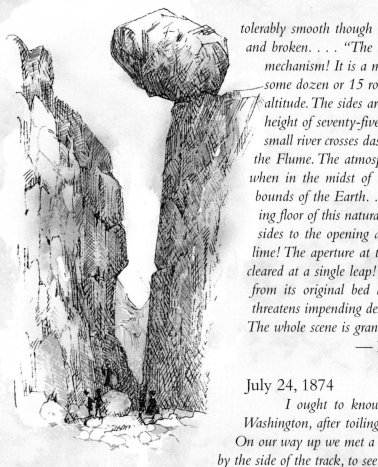

tolerably smooth though the ground over which it passes is rocky and broken. . . . "The Flume" is a stupendous piece of natural mechanism! It is a massive gorge or chasm in the mountains, some dozen or 15 rods in length and from 8 to twelve feet in altitude. The sides are solid rock, rising perpendicularly to the height of seventy-five feet from the bottom where we stood. A small river crosses dashing and foaming over the rocks through the Flume. The atmosphere is damp and humid and one feels when in the midst of the rocks as if he were engulfed in the bounds of the Earth. . . . As the beholden stands on the rocking floor of this natural mill "Flume" and gazes up, the granite sides to the opening above are peculiarly impressive and sublime! The aperture at the top seems so narrow that it could be cleared at a single leap! And a large boulder which has tumbled from its original bed has lodged between the two sides, and threatens impending destruction to one who stood gazing below. The whole scene is grand and sublimely impressive!

— From the diary of Mason Tappan

July 24, 1874

I ought to know something about the measurement of Washington, after toiling up that rail road track to the top. . . . On our way up we met a train coming down, and sat upon a rock by the side of the track, to see it pass. The first intimation of its approach which we had was a sound which very much resembled that made by a moving machine. As the train approached we saw that the baggage car was ahead, the engine next, and the car for passengers behind. The train moves very slowly, taking about an hour and a half to make a passage either up or down. When we go up again, we resolve, we will take the car. But we were much amused by the general appearance of the car's passengers: A more pale, silent, frightened looking set of people, I never saw. . . . Most of them sat looking apprehensively at one another at every sound; arms folded, speechless, perhaps "preparing themselves" for the catastrophe, which all rules of mechanics would tell them is impossible. I am glad I had this experience. I never before saw such an exhibition of the sentiment of terror.

— From *How Frank and I Spent Two Weeks in the White Mountains of New Hampshire* by F. W. Sanborn

A Rugged Recipe from the Granite State

Every year, thousands of people who love the outdoors flock to New Hampshire, eager to hike the rugged mountain trails. You can bet plenty of those hikers are snacking on trail mix along the way. The best thing about this recipe is that you get to choose the ingredients.

White Mountain Trail Mix

You will need a large plastic bag you can close tightly.
Choose two ingredients from each of the following categories:
- Something salty: peanuts, pretzels, sunflower seeds, or popcorn
- Something sweet: chocolate chips, butterscotch chips, M&M's, Reese's Pieces, gummy bears, or banana chips
- Something chewy: raisins, dried cranberries, or dried apricots cut into small pieces
- Cereal: Cheerios, Wheat Chex, or granola

Place a quarter cup of each ingredient you choose into the bag. Close the bag tightly and shake it up.
Makes two cups.
Happy trails!